"Are we nearly there yet?"

Poems About Journeys

Chosen by Gervase Phinn

W
FRANKLIN WATTS
LONDON•SYDNEY

First published in 2001 by
Franklin Watts
96 Leonard Street
London
EC2A 4XD

Franklin Watts Australia
56 O'Riordan Street
Alexandria
NSW 2015

A CIP catalogue record for this book is available
from the British Library.

ISBN 0 7496 4085 5

Series Editor: Louise John
Designer: Robert Walster

Dewey Classification 821.008

Printed in Hong Kong

Acknowledgments

The editor and publishers gratefully acknowledge permission to reproduce the following
copyright material.

'Let Basil Go to Basildon' by Colin West. © Colin West. Reprinted with permission of
the author.
'Seaside Song' by John Rice. © John Rice. Reprinted with permission of the author.
'Yesterday Our Family Visited The Seashore' by Ian Souter. © Ian Souter. Reprinted by
permission of the author.
'The Longest Journey In The World' by Michael Rosen. © 1980 Michael Rosen.
Reprinted by permission of Peters Fraser & Dunlop on behalf of Michael Rosen.
'Flying' by Kaye Starbird, from 'Don't Ever Cross a Crocodile. Copyright © 1963, 1991
by Kaye Starbird. Used by permission of Marian Reiner.
'All Aboard!' By Judith Nicholls, from 'Wish You Were Here?' By Judith Nicholls
published by Oxford University Press. © Judith Nicholls 1992. Reprinted by permission
of the author.
'Lullaby' by Alan Bold. Copyright © Alan Bold. Reprinted by permission of Alice Bold.
Extract from 'My Ship' by Christy Brown, from 'Collected Poems (Come Softly to My
Wake) by Christy Brown, published by Secker & Warburg. Used by permission of The
Random House Group Limited.
'I Don't Want to Live on the Moon' by Jeff Moss, from 'The Butterfly Jar'. © Jeff Moss.
Reprinted by permission of International Creative Management Inc.
'Night Train' by Irene Rawnsley, from 'Night Poems' edited by John Foster, published by
Oxford University Press, 1991. Reprinted by permission of the author.
'It Has Been a Very Bad Day' by John Foster. © 2001 John Foster. Included by
permission of the author.
'Who Is You?' By Rony Robinson, from 'A Fifth Poetry Book' published by Oxford
University Press. © 1985 Rony Robinson. Reprinted by permission of Peters Fraser &
Dunlop on behalf of Rony Robinson.
'Where's Melissa?' By David R. Morgan. Reprinted by permission of the author.
'Stopping by Woods on a Snowy Evening' by Robert Frost, from 'The Poetry of Robert
Frost' edited by Edward Connery Lathem, the Estate of Robert Frost and Jonathan Cape
as publisher. Used by permission of The Random House Group Limited.
'White Fields' by James Stephens. Reprinted by permission of The Society of Authors as
the Literary Representatives of the Estate of James Stephens.
'Star Gazing' by Gareth Owen, from 'Collected Poems for Children' published by
Macmillan Books. Copyright © Gareth Owen 1994. Reprinted by permission of the
author c/o Rogers, Coleridge & White Ltd., 20 Powis Mews, London W11 1JN.
'Lower the Diver' by Richard Edwards, from 'The House That Caught a Cold'
published by Puffin in 1993. © Richard Edwards. Reprinted with permission of the
author.
'A Flock of Little Boats' by Samuel Menashe, republished in 'Penguin Modern Poets
Volume 7'. Reprinted by permission of the author.

Every effort has been made to trace copyright, but if any omissions have been made,
please let us know in order that this may be corrected in the next edition.

Picture Credits

Bach-Grahammer/Britstock-IFA: 17
Jonathan Blair/Corbis: 30-31
Britstock-IFA: 6
Bruce Coleman Inc/Bruce Coleman Collection: 9
Robert Dowling/ Corbis: 4-5
Warren Faidley/OSF: cover, 1, 2
G Grafenhain/Britstock-IFA: 24-25
Charles Gupton/Corbis Stockmarket: 27
Lester Lefkowitz/Corbis Stockmarket: 21
Romilly Lockyer/Image Bank: 7
Russell Manson/Corbis Stockmarket: 12
Karen Huntt Mason/Corbis: 11
Mug Shots/Corbis Stockmarket: 28-29
NASA/Photodisc: 18-19
Jules Perrier/Corbis Stockmarket: 16
Hans Reinhard/Bruce Coleman Collection: 8
Norbert Schafer/Corbis Stockmarket: 23
Pete Turner/Image Bank: 20
Larry Williams/Corbis Stockmarket: 14-15

Contents

Let Basil Go to Basildon

Let Basil go to Basildon,
Let Lester go to Leicester;
Let Steven go to Stevenage
With raincoat and sou'wester.

Let Peter go to Peterhead,
Let Dudley go to Dudley;
Let Milton go to Milton Keynes –
The pavements there are puddly.

Let Felix go to Felixstowe,
Let Barry go to Barry;
Let Mabel go to Mablethorpe,
But I at home shall tarry.

Let Alice go to Alice Springs,
Let Florence go to Florence;
Let Benny go to Benidorm
Where rain comes down in torrents.

Let Winnie go to Winnipeg,
Let Sidney go to Sydney;
Let Otto go to Ottawa –
I am not of that kidney.

Let Vera go to Veracruz,
Let Nancy go to Nancy,
But I'll stay home while others roam –
Abroad I do not fancy.

Colin West

Yesterday Our Family Visited the Seashore!

Yesterday our family visited the seashore
To search for sea creatures and a whole lot more.
But all we found were
A squashed-up drink can,
A plastic toy made in Japan,
A length of fishing line,
A punctured football, just like mine,
A soggy cigarette packet,
A smashed-up old tennis racket,
A child's yellow beach shoe,
A screwed-up dirty tissue,
  A coil of rusty wire,
      A black rubber car tyre,
         A piece of food in kitchen foil,
           And a rockpool full of thick filthy oil.
            All this in one morning on the seashore,
            A whole lot of pollution
               and not much more!

Ian Souter

Seaside Song

It was a
sun-boiled, bright light, fried egg, hot skin, sun-tanned
ssssizzzzzzler of a day.

It was a
pop song, ding-dong, candy floss, dodgem car, arcade, no shade
smashing seaside town.

We had
a well time, a swell time, a real pell-mell time,
a fine time, a rhyme time, a super double-dime time.

We
beach swam, ate ham, gobbled up a chicken leg,
climbed trees, chased bees,
got stuck in sand up to our knees,
played chase, flew in space,
beat a seagull in a skating race,
rowed boats, quenched throats,
spent a load of £5 notes,
sang songs, hummed tunes,
played hide and seek in sandy dunes.

Did all these things
too much by far
that we fell asleep going back in the car
from the seaside.

John Rice

Windy Nights

Rumbling in the chimneys,
Rattling at the doors.
Round the roofs and round the roads
The rude wind roars;
Raging through the darkness,
Raving through the trees,
Racing off again across
The great grey seas.

Rodney Bennett

Up-hill

Does the road wind up-hill all the way?
    Yes, to the very end.
Will the day's journey take the whole long day?
    From morn to night, my friend.

But is there for the night a resting-place?
    A roof for when the slow dark hours begin.
May not the darkness hide it from my face?
    You cannot miss that inn.

Shall I meet other wayfarers at night?
    Those who have gone before.
Then must I knock or call when just in sight?
    They will not keep you standing at the door.

Shall I find comfort, travel-sore and weak?
    Of labour you shall find the sum.
Will there be beds for me and all who seek?
    Yea, beds for all who come.

Christina Rossetti

The Longest Journey in the World

'Last one into bed
has to switch out the light.'
It's just the same every night.
There's a race.
I'm ripping off my trousers and shirt,
he's kicking off his shoes and socks.

'My sleeve's stuck.'
'This button's too big for its button-hole.'
'Have you hidden my pyjamas?'
'Keep your hands off mine.'

If you win
you get where it's safe
before the darkness comes –
but if you lose
if you're last
you know what you've got coming up is
the journey from the light switch to your bed.
It's the Longest Journey in the World.

'You're last tonight,' my brother says.
And he's right.

There is nowhere so dark
as that room in the moment
after I've switched out the light.

There is nowhere so full of dangerous things,
things that love dark places,

things that breathe only when you breathe
and hold their breath when I hold mine.

So I have to say:
'I'm not scared.'
That face, grinning in the pattern on the wall,
isn't a face –
'I'm not scared.'
That prickle on the back of my neck
is only the label on my pyjama jacket –
'I'm not scared.'
That moaning-moaning is nothing
but water in a pipe –
'I'm not scared.'

Everything's going to be just fine
as soon as I get into that bed of mine.
Such a terrible shame
It's always the same
It takes so long
It takes so long
It takes so long
to get there.

From the light switch
to my bed
It's the Longest Journey in the World.

Michael Rosen

Flying

I like to ride in my uncle's plane,
The one he pilots around the sky.
It's little and blue
And shiny, too,
And looks a lot like a dragonfly.

And once we're high in the summer air
With things below all shrunken in size,
It's easy to dream
How life would seem
If human beings were dragonflies.

The great wide river shrinks to a brook
That slowly winds away to the north,
Where ferries and tugs
Are water bugs
That skitter silently back and forth.

The faraway cows are just like ants,
And woods are patches of gray-green moss,
And telegraph lines
Where sunlight shines
Are glinting spider webs strung across.

It's quite exciting to hum through space
And view the world with an insect's eye.
A dragonfly-view
Makes things seem new,
Unless, of course, you're a dragonfly.

Kaye Starbird

All Aboard!

Hurry, scurry, in the car!
Push that dog down, lock the door!
Where's my bucket? In the boot;
Move that deckchair off my foot!

Are we in now? Wait a minute,
Here's a shoe with no one in it!
Bats and buckets, spades and balls,
Plastic macs for sudden squalls ...

Hurry, scurry; lock the door!
Get that dog down on the floor!
Hurry, scurry; wait for me!
Who'll be first to see the sea?

Food and chairs and picnic bag,
Grandpa, Sue, the boys, the dog;
Mum with maps and sandwich box,
Dad white-legged in winter socks ...

Hurry, scurry; lock that door —
this poor car will take no more!
Hurry, scurry; turn the key,
we're off at last to see the sea!

Judith Nicholls

Lullaby

Close your eyes gently
    And cuddle in
Keep yourself snug, a
    New day will begin.

Have pleasant dreams about
    Those things you love,
Sleep is an island
    Waiting above.

Night is a blanket
    Keeping you warm
If you close your eyes you can
    Come to no harm.

Dreams are like journeys
    Drifting along,
Rest is a present
    Keeping you strong.

Alan Bold

My Ship

When I was a lad my bed was the ship
that voyaged me far through the star-dusted night
to lands forever beyond the world's lip
dark burning olive lands of delight
across blood-red oceans under the stars
lorded by the scarlet splendour of Mars.

It is only a bed now spread with eiderdown
and the sheets merciless chains holding me down.

Christy Brown

I Don't Want to Live on the Moon

I'd like to visit the moon
On a rocket ship high in the air.
Yes, I'd like to visit the moon,
But I don't think I'd like to live there.
Though I'd like to look down at the earth from above,
I would miss all the places and people I love.
So although I might like it for one afternoon
I don't want to live on the moon.

I'd like to travel under the sea,
I could meet all the fish everywhere.
Yes, I'd travel under the sea,
But I don't think I'd like to live there.
I might stay for a day if I had my wish,
But there's not much to do when your friends are all fish,
And an oyster and clam aren't real family,
So I don't want to live in the sea.

I'd like to visit the jungle, hear the lion roar,
Go back in time and meet a dinosaur.
There are so many strange places I'd like to be,
But none of them permanently.

So if I should visit the moon,
I will dance on a moonbeam and then
I will make a wish on a star,
And I'll wish I was home once again.
Though I'd like to look down at the earth from above,
I would miss all the places and people I love.
So although I may go, I'll be coming home soon,
'Cause I don't want to live on the moon.

Jeff Moss

18

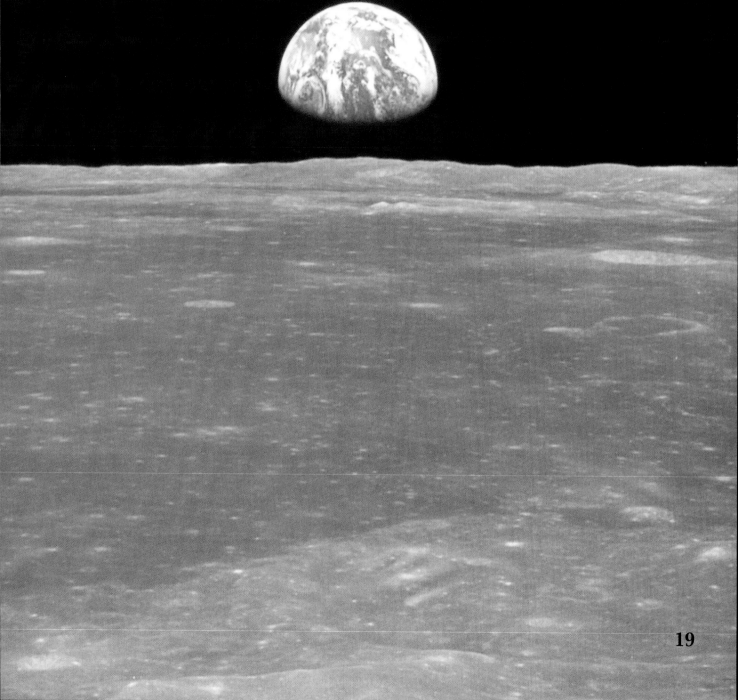

19

From a Railway Carriage

Faster than fairies, faster than witches,
Bridges and houses, hedges and ditches;
And charging along like troops in a battle,
All through the meadows the horses and cattle;
All of the sights of the hill and the plain
Fly as thick as driving rain;
And ever again, in the wink of an eye,
Painted stations whistle by.

Here is a child who clambers and scrambles,
All by himself and gathering brambles;
Here is a tramp who stands and gazes;
And there is the green for stringing the daisies!
Here is a cart run away in the road
Lumping along with man and load;
And here is a mill, and there is a river:
Each a glimpse and gone for ever!

Robert Louis Stevenson

Night Train

The train
Is a shiny caterpillar
In clackity boots
Nosing through the blind night,
Munching mile after mile
Of darkness.

Irene Rawnsley

A Peanut

A peanut sat on the railway track,
His heart was all a-flutter.
Along came a train, the 10.15 –
Toot-toot! – peanut butter!

American Rhyme

Leaving Home

When Matthew was seven,
He decided to leave home.
He packed his little bag
And tucked his teddy underneath his arm,
And said, 'I'm going. I've had enough.'
'Why are you leaving, Matty?' asked Dad.
'Because you shouted at me.'
'No I didn't. I never raised my voice.'
'You shouted at me with your eyes,' said Matthew.
'Shall I run you to the station?' asked Dad.
'No, I'll get a bus.'
'Well, goodbye then, Matty,' said Dad opening the door
Onto the cold, black night beyond.
Matthew peered into the darkness.
'And be careful of the wolves,' said Dad.
'I'm not going now,' replied Matthew.
'I've changed my mind.'

Gervase Phinn

It Has Been a Very Bad Day

It has been a very bad day.
I fell in the dirt and tore my new shirt.
I thought that I might run away.
But my favourite cartoon's on TV
And there's ice cream and jelly for tea
So I have decided to stay.

John Foster

22

23

Stopping by Woods on a Snowy Evening

Whose woods these are I think I know.
His house is in the village though;
He will not see me stopping here
To watch his woods fill up with snow.

My little horse must think it queer
To stop without a farmhouse near
Between the woods and frozen lake
The darkest evening of the year.

He gives his harness bells a shake
To ask if there is some mistake.
The only other sound's the sweep
Of easy wind and downy flake.

The woods are lovely, dark and deep,
But I have promises to keep,
And miles to go before I sleep,
And miles to go before I sleep.

Robert Frost

White Fields

In the winter time we go
Walking in the fields of snow;
Where there is no grass at all;
Where the top of every wall,
Every fence, and every tree
Is as white as white can be.
Pointing out the way we came –
Every one of them the same –
All across the fields there be
Prints in silver filigree;
And our mothers always know,
By the footprints in the snow,
Where it is the children go.

James Stephens

Who is You?

Let's all climb the family tree
See who's you and who is me.

If you are your brother's brother,
Your grandad's daughter is your mother.
But while we're finding who is who
Your grandad's little girl's little girl's you.

If you're a girl climbing family trees,
Your father's brother calls you niece.
He calls you nephew if you're a lad,
But says 'Hi brother!' to your dad.

Now the family tree is buzzing,
Your brother's sister's kid's your cousin.
Your nephew's uncle's you you see,
And my father's brother's nephew's me.

The more we climb the more the fun,
Your great grandma's grandad's mum.
And here's something else you'll find is true,
Your sister's baby's uncle's you.

Up the tree, oh this is the life,
Grandma's daughter-in-law's uncle's wife.
Let's all climb the family tree,
If you're your mum's only child, you're me.

Rony Robinson

Where's Melissa?

Melissa dreamt that she could fly
Like a bird-girl in the sky,
She took with her a diamond spoon
To eat the cherry-pancake moon.

David R Morgan

Star Gazing

At midnight through my window
I spy with wondering eye
The far-off stars and planets
Sprinkled on the sky.

There the constant North Star
Hangs above our trees
And there the Plough and Sirius
And the distant Pleiades.

Star on star past counting
Each one a raging sun
And the sky one endless suburb
With all her lights left on.

How strange it is that certain stars
Whose distant lights still glow
Vanished in that sea of space
Three million years ago.

And if I stare too long a time
The stars swim in my eyes
Drifting towards my bedroom
Down the vast slopes of the sky.

And, mesmerised, I wonder,
Will *our* Earth someday die?
Spreading her fabric and her dreams
In fragments on the sky.

And then my imagination
Sees in some distant dawn
A young girl staring skywards
On a planet still unborn.

And will she also wonder,
Was there ever life out there?
Before the whole thing vanished
Like a dream into the air.

Gareth Owen

Lower the Diver

Lower the diver over the side,
Down to the roots of the swirling tide.

Lower the diver, weighted with lead,
Glass and brass helmet over his head.

Lower the diver on to the deck
And the barnacled masts of the long-lost wreck.

Lower the diver; will he find jars,
Rust-sealed treasure-chests, silver bars?

Lower the diver; will he find gold,
Cannon-balls, skulls or an empty hold?

Lower the diver; pray that the shark
Doesn't mind guests in the salty dark.

Lower the diver; then man the winch,
Wind him up slowly, inch by inch.

Undo his helmet. Why does he weep?
Is it so bad to be hauled from the deep?

Talk to the diver. What does he mean —
'Mermaids are real and her eyes were green'?

Richard Edwards

A Flock of Little Boats

A flock of little boats
Tethered to the shore
Drifts in still water...
Prows dip, nibbling.

Samuel Menashe

A Good Play

We built a ship upon the stairs
All made of the back-bedroom chairs,
And filled it full of sofa pillows
To go a-sailing on the billows.

We took a saw and several nails,
And water in the nursery pails;
And Tom said, 'Let us also take
An apple and a slice of cake;'
Which was enough for Tom and me
To go a-sailing on, till tea.

We sailed along for days and days,
And had the very best of plays;
But Tom fell out and hurt his knee,
So there was no one left but me.

Robert Louis Stevenson

Index of First Lines